BRITISH MUSEUM PAPER PAGEANTS
ROMANS

Designed and illustrated by
BEVERLY SAUNDERS

JONATHAN CAPE
in association with
BRITISH MUSEUM PUBLICATIONS

INTRODUCTION

At its height, the Roman Empire was enormous and extremely powerful. Its provinces surrounded the Mediterranean Sea, stretching from Egypt to Britain and from the Middle East to Spain. In control of this huge territory was the Roman Emperor. He commanded the Roman army and was chief magistrate of Rome. His power and importance were so great that he was often honoured as a god; temples which had been dedicated to him could be found in most provinces.

To govern so many different lands and peoples was a formidable undertaking, so some standard measures were introduced throughout the Empire. The *pax romana*, or state of peace, was imposed on each new province, and army and government officials were made responsible for law and order.

A standard system of weights and measures, money and taxation was developed. A network of well-made roads was established, and new ports were opened to link every corner of the Empire. Trade flourished, and soon Rome became the wealthiest city the world had ever seen, enjoying luxuries from all her provinces.

In return, Roman ideas, fashions and the Latin language spread widely through the provinces. Most citizens soon became accustomed to Roman ways.

This book shows you what life might have been like in the Roman Empire nearly two thousand years ago. There are four scenes, two set in Rome, the centre of the Empire, and two in Britain, an important Roman province.

SCENE 1: THE FORUM

The forum was the commercial, legal and social centre of the Roman city. It was a large open space used for markets and public meetings. Surrounding it on two sides were shopping arcades and offices. At each end of the forum were usually the *basilica* (the law courts) and the *curia*, where the town council met.

This scene shows what one corner of the forum might have been like in the early morning. Two shops have just pulled up their wooden shutters. They will close in the afternoon when it gets too hot, and open again in the evening.

The draper has set out his fabrics and cushions, hoping to attract slaves sent out to shop by their wealthy mistresses. The bronzesmith's wife is arranging her wares on the simple wooden counter, whilst in a small workshop behind her husband makes more jugs, scales and oil lamps to sell.

Upstairs in the cramped one-room flats some early risers watch two women chatting below their balconies. One has just bought fresh bread from the public bakery, which she is sharing with her neighbour. As *plebeians*, the lowest rank of Roman inhabitant, they are too poor to own ovens themselves.

In the centre of the forum, market stalls selling fruit and vegetables, fresh meat and fish, crocks and pots, have been set up. A keen inspector (an *aedile*) is making sure that the grape-seller is not cheating his customers. He has not noticed that the grape-seller's assistant has rushed off to borrow money from the money-lender.

All the stall-holders collected their fresh produce from the warehouses near the docks, and brought it into the city in carts during the night to avoid traffic jams. A young slave is still unloading cooking pots and *amphorae*. He is late – no carts are allowed in the forum after sunrise.

Three *senators* (members of the governing body) arrive at the curia, ready to spend a long day discussing government policies and deciding how best to spend public money. Near by, a teacher tries to make a group of sleepy boys understand arithmetic – he has to shout above the noise of the now busy forum.

As the day gets warmer, people gather round the public fountain to exchange news.

SCENE 2: THE COLOSSEUM

The Colosseum was a huge stone amphitheatre in Rome, built especially for the Games. It had tiers of seats arranged around a central arena in which the Games took place.

The Games were gruesome fights which were held by the Emperor's officials to entertain the Roman citizens on public holidays. Non-citizens were not allowed to attend. Enormous crowds flocked to these bloodthirsty spectacles, eager to watch desperate gladiators and wild beasts fight to the death.

This scene shows what they might have watched. The audience has already enjoyed an impressive gladiatorial procession, accompanied by dancers, jugglers, musicians and priests. The opening combats with wild animals are over, and a *bestiarius* gladiator is dragged away from the ferocious lions. The blood left in the arena is hurriedly covered with sand.

Excitement mounts as lots are drawn for the main fights. The crowds are placing their bets, and want to find out who will be drawn to fight against their favourite gladiators.

A *myrmillo* gladiator, who has an oval shield to protect him, is drawn against a muscular *Samnite* sporting an impressive plumed helmet and large, rectangular shield. A *retiarius* gladiator, with only his net and trident, is set against a well-armed *Thracian*.

All of them are slaves, prisoners-of-war or criminals, who have been rigorously trained to fight in one of Rome's special gladiatorial schools.

A war trumpet (*tuba*) heralds the gladiators as they greet the Emperor, crying,

"Hail, Emperor, those about to die salute you."

The battle begins, accompanied by music from a small organ. Suddenly, the Thracian staggers to the ground, trapped in the retiarius's net. The defeated Thracian throws aside his shield in surrender.

All eyes turn to the Emperor in anticipation. He signals with his thumb – the Thracian's life is to be spared.

The retiarius gladiator is carried around the arena in triumph, much to the delight of his loyal supporters. If he continues to win, he will soon be able to buy his freedom.

SCENE 3: HADRIAN'S WALL

Though others before him had thought of doing so, it was the Emperor Claudius who added Britain to the Roman Empire. The army of invasion which he sent across the English Channel consisted of four legions, together with many smaller units of auxiliary soldiers – altogether some 40,000–50,000 highly trained soldiers.

In the south people seem to have adapted gradually to Roman ways, even learning to speak Latin, but further north resistance to the invaders was greater and lasted longer. Some tribes were particularly hostile to Rome and preferred to live as they had always done.

In time it became clear that the whole of Britain could not be conquered successfully, so the Emperor Hadrian decreed that a fortified frontier should be constructed. Hadrian's Wall was built to separate and protect the province of *Britannia* from the warlike tribes of northern England and Scotland. Soldiers were garrisoned along the Wall in forts and "mile castles", from where they carried out patrols, joining forces in case of serious attacks.

Although Britain was a Roman province for nearly four centuries, peace was never so certain that the army could be removed completely from Hadrian's Wall. Gradually, however, local inhabitants became accustomed to 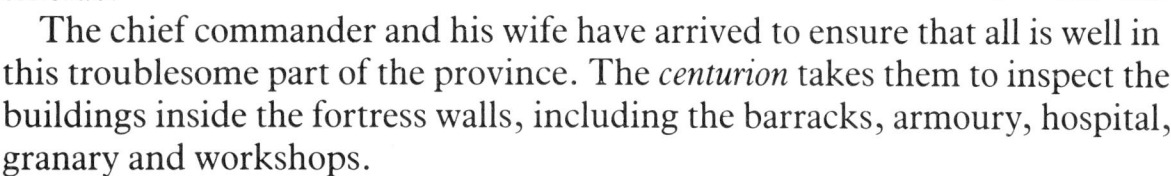 the soldiers. Some left their villages and settled outside the forts, opening small shops and taverns to make a living from the well-paid troops. Fresh vegetables, corn and meat were exchanged for money, or offered instead of taxes.

This scene shows what part of a *vicus* (settlement) might have been like.

Three soldiers are recovering after several days' marching through howling winds and driving rain. They are used to being posted to remote frontiers of the Empire. None of them are *legionaries*, the best-paid Roman soldiers, because they are not Roman citizens. Instead, all three have become *auxiliaries*, enticed by the prospect of earning citizenship and all its privileges after twenty-five years of loyal service. Now, after their journey, they must polish their dirty bronze helmets, and clean their mail tunics and leather-covered shields.

The chief commander and his wife have arrived to ensure that all is well in this troublesome part of the province. The *centurion* takes them to inspect the buildings inside the fortress walls, including the barracks, armoury, hospital, granary and workshops.

A despatch rider is sent to warn the neighbouring fort of the commander's arrival. It will be a long, hard ride. The horse is loaded with a leather satchel containing a warm cloak, a bronze cooking pot and a net of bread, onions and salt fish.

In the tavern opposite, two off-duty soldiers enjoy a game of dice. They look forward to their retirement when they can marry and settle in the vicus.

In the background the villagers have brought corn, fruit and fresh mutton. The soldiers are pleased – supper will be more interesting this evening.

SCENE 4: A ROMANO-BRITISH VILLA

Villas in Roman Britain were country houses, normally part of a farm. Although many were simple and modest, some were impressive buildings at the heart of large estates. More than money, the ownership of land, particularly agricultural land, was the measure of wealth and status in the Roman world. The rich owner of a big estate might spend only part of the year at his villa, living the rest of the time in a near-by town. The running of the farm and estate would then be the responsibility of a *vilicus* (bailiff).

This scene shows what one of the richer villas of Roman Britain might have been like. The owner has carefully chosen the site, building the villa on a sunny, south-facing slope near a river. Wide, well-made roads, first built many years ago by the Roman army, make it easy for him or his bailiff to reach the town to sell produce and hire more labourers.

New farming methods and implements have improved the farm's productivity. A heavier plough and two-handled scythe have made ploughing and harvesting much easier.

Better breeds of sheep and cattle graze in the pastures. New crops, including carrots and celery, grow in the fields, and lush orchards produce apples, cherries, nuts and pears. If the year has been a good one, the surplus will be big enough to yield a sizeable profit, even after taxes have been paid.

The profits of many previous years have enabled the owner to improve his living quarters. Influenced by continental villas, he has added two side-wings to the main building. One is for his children, now grown up. The other houses a vilicus and his family. Inside the main building, the owner's wife has had the floors decorated with colourful mosaics and the walls with beautiful paintings. The new side-wings form an enclosed courtyard. This was once part of the muddy farmyard. It is now an ornate, walled garden with a fountain at its centre.

In the farmyard opposite, labourers tend the geese and hens. Their wives patiently weave baskets for the crops. Labourers pile the harvested *spelt* (wheat) and barley into wooden carts to carry them in from the fields. They work from dawn to dusk every day of the week, and are now looking forward to the harvest festival – a time to rest from their hard work and celebrate.

Near by the residential craftsmen are busy in the estate's workshops. The carpenter mends fences, gates and furniture, while the thatcher is repairing the shed's leaking roof. The tanner busily beats the cattle hides – they will be sold at the market for shoes and clothing. Next door the blacksmith hammers at his anvil, making new tools and mending broken farm implements. Outside the potter makes storage jars for the estate honey and other farm produce, and new kitchen utensils for the owner's wife.

The villa owner treats his loyal workers well. He knows that without their skill and dedication he would not enjoy such an efficient and productive estate.

Strip D. Glue villa-scene Side-piece C along here

Glue here

Cut along

Cut along

Cut along

Fold

Fold

Fold back and glue to the Roman forum floor

Fold

Fold back and glue to Roman-Britain villa floor Strip A

JVLIAM AMO

Cut along

Cut along ✂

Fold back and glue to Hadrian's Wall-scene floor.

Fold

Fold

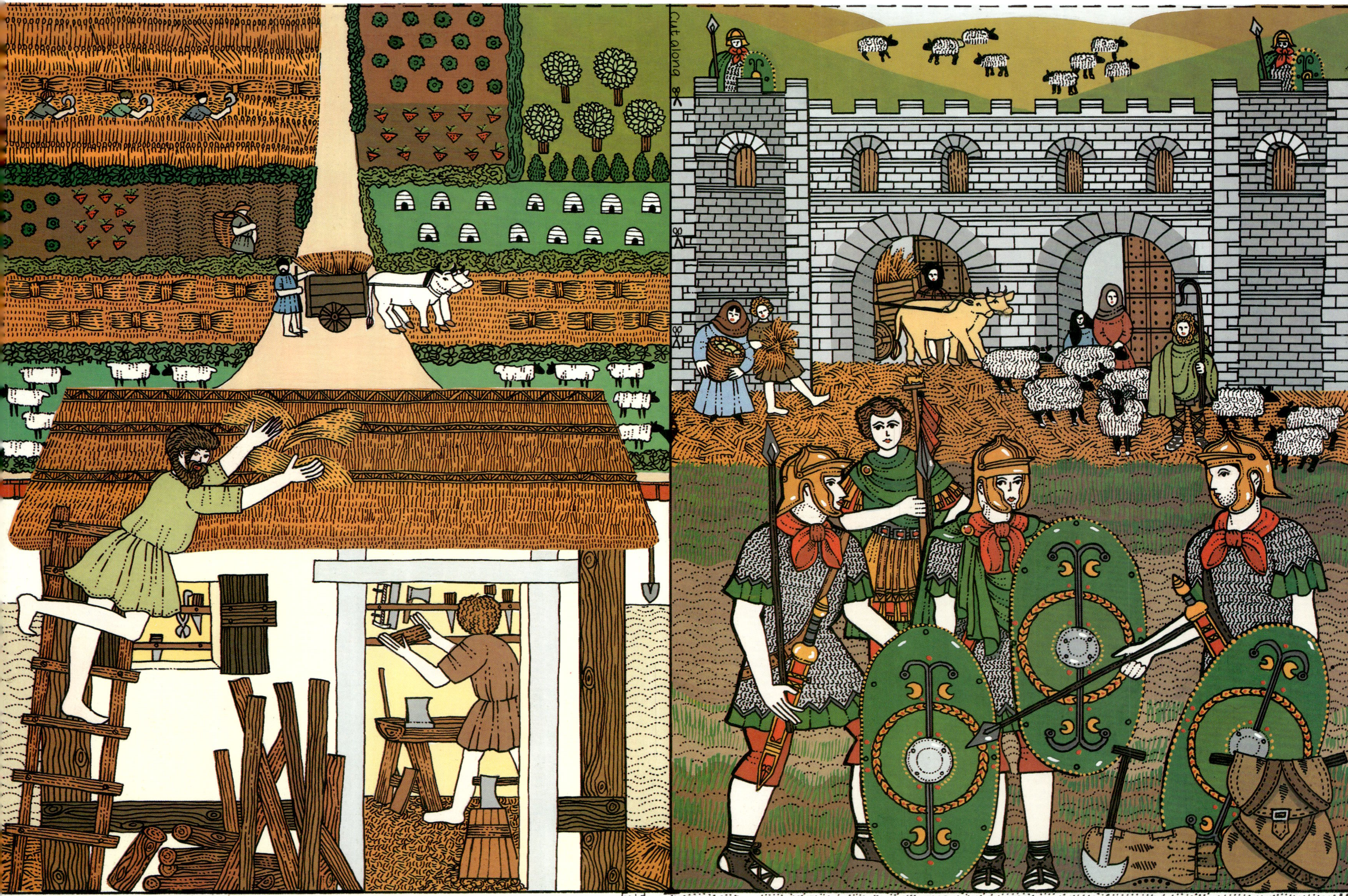

Fold

Fold back and glue to the gladiator-scene floor.

Fold

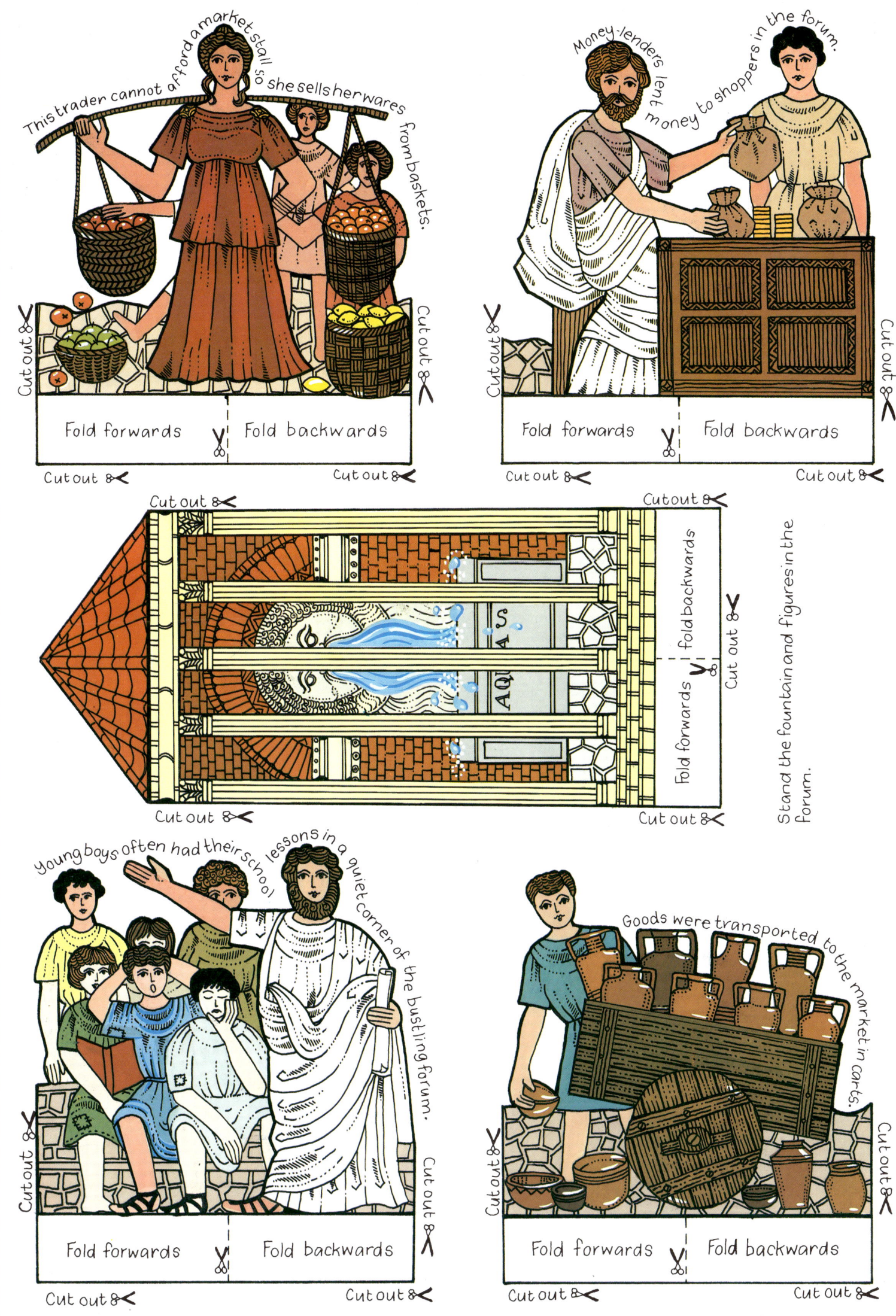

This trader cannot afford a market stall so she sells her wares from baskets.

Cut out &✂

Cut out &✂

Fold forwards ✂ Fold backwards

Cut out &✂

Cut out &✂

Money-lenders lent money to shoppers in the forum.

Cut out &✂

Cut out &✂

Fold forwards ✂ Fold backwards

Cut out &✂

Cut out &✂

Cut out &✂

Cut out &✂

AQUA S

Fold forwards ✂ Fold backwards

Stand the fountain and figures in the Forum.

Cut out &✂

Cut out &✂

Young boys often had their school lessons in a quiet corner of the bustling forum.

Cut out &✂

Cut out &✂

Fold forwards ✂ Fold backwards

Cut out &✂

Cut out &✂

Goods were transported to the market in carts.

Cut out &✂

Cut out &✂

Fold forwards ✂ Fold backwards

Cut out &✂

Cut out &✂

Cut out ✂ Cut out ✂

Fold

Cut out ✂ Cut out ✂

Fold forwards Fold backwards

Cut out ✂ Cut out ✂

Cut out these market stalls. Fold them down the middle where marked. Stand them in the busy forum.

Cut out ✂ Cut out ✂

Fold

Cut out ✂ Cut out ✂

Fold forwards Fold backwards

Cut out ✂ Cut out ✂

Fold this strip in half.
Cut slots where marked.

Fold

Slot underneath the gladiator to
form a triangular stand behind him.

Cut out

Cut out

Cut out

Cut out

Cut out

A Samnite gladiator always wore a plumed helmet and carried a large shield.

Stand the gladiators and lions in the Colosseum, where the Emperor and his wife can watch them fight.

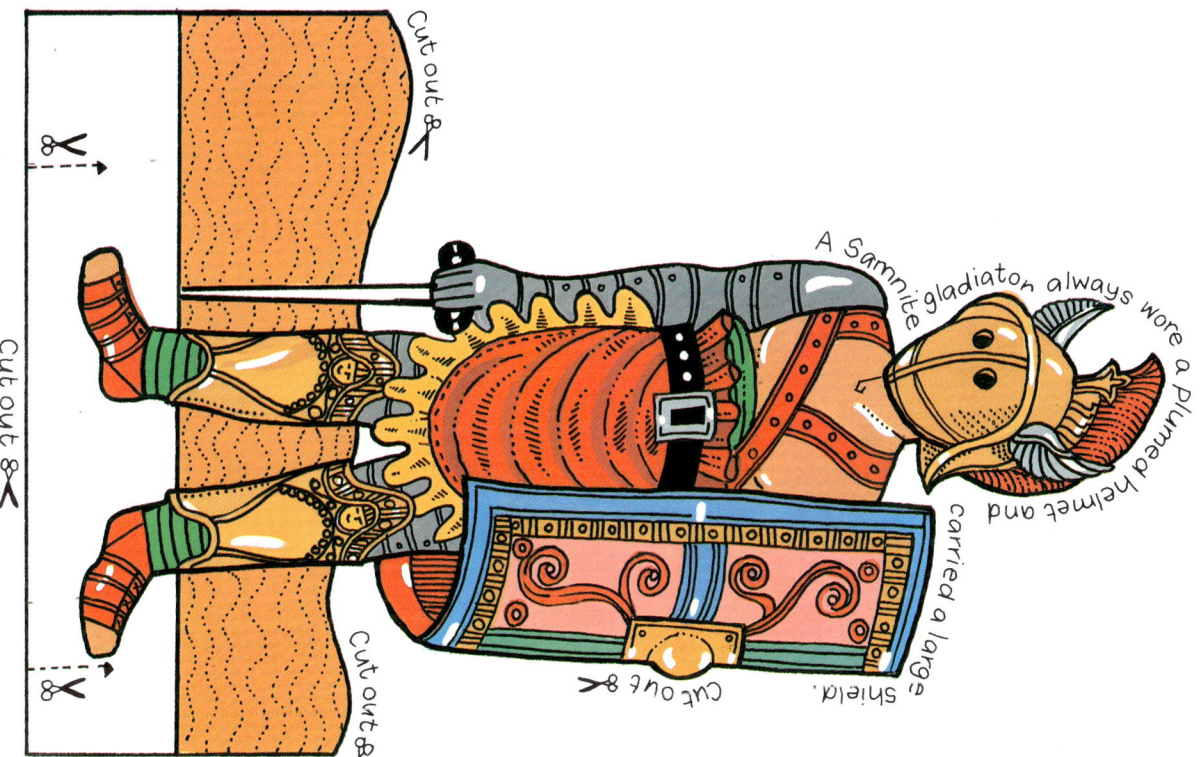

This bestiarius gladiator has just lost his battle against these two fearsome lions.

Cut out

Cut out

Fold forwards

Fold backwards

Cut out

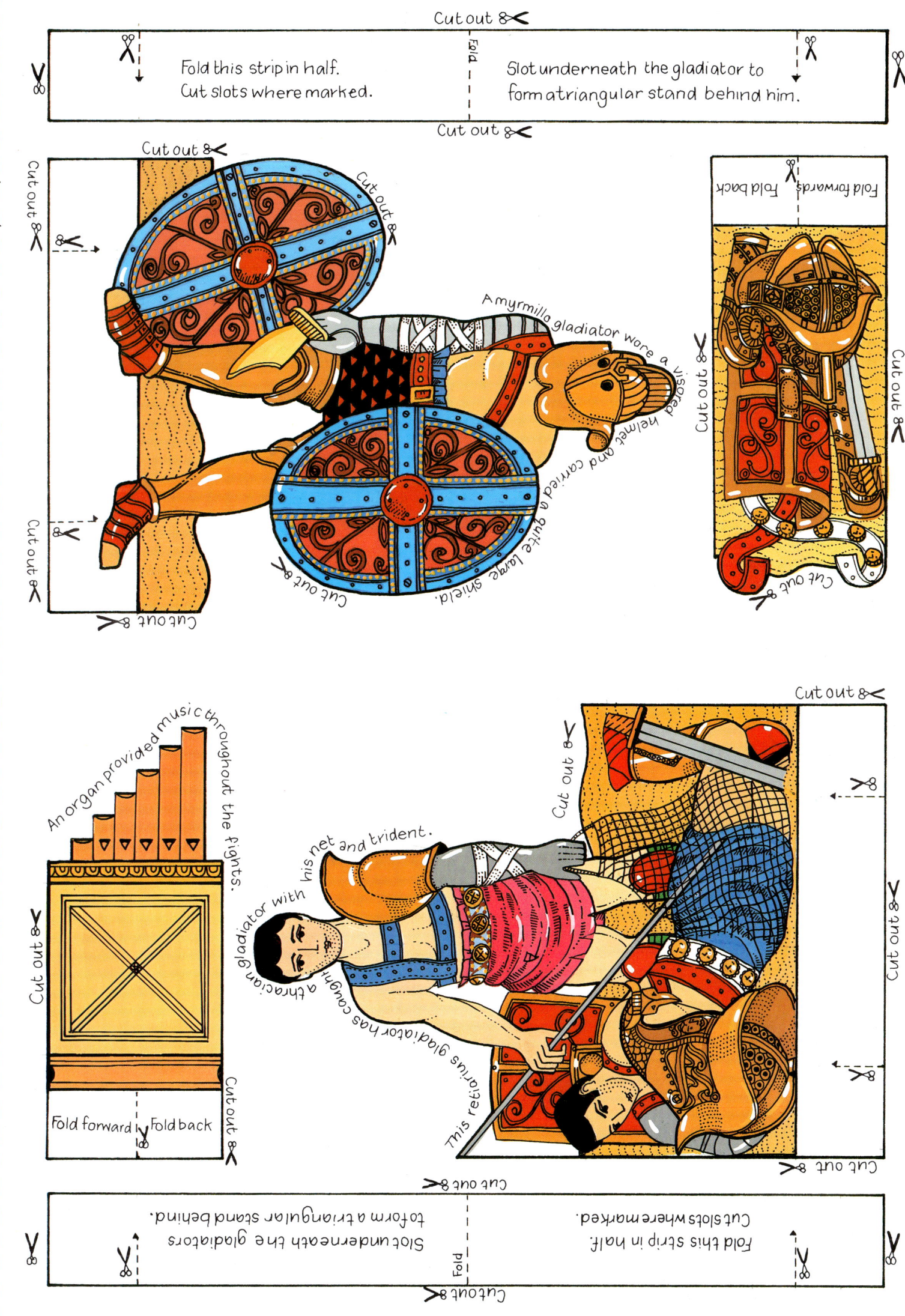

Cut out &

Fold this strip in half.
Cut slots where marked.

Slot underneath the gladiator to form a triangular stand behind him.

Cut out &

Cut out &

A myrmillo gladiator wore a visored helmet and carried a quite large shield.

An organ provided music throughout the fights.

A Thracian gladiator with his net and trident.

This retiarius gladiator has caught his...

Fold forward   Fold back

Slot underneath the gladiators to form a triangular stand behind.

Fold this strip in half.
Cut slots where marked.

Fold back ✂ Fold forwards ✂ Fold forwards

Cut out ✂

Cut out ✂

The commanding officer was the most important soldier at the fort.

Cut out ✂

Fold forwards ✂ Fold back

Cut out ✂

Cut out ✂

Fold forwards ✂ Fold back

Cut out ✂

The centurion was a hard taskmaster who kept his soldiers in order.

Cut out ✂

The commanding officer's wife

Cut out ✂

Stand these figures in the civilian settlement outside Hadrian's Wall.

This soldier has just returned from scouting duty along the wall.

Cut out ✂

Cut out ✂

Cut out ✂

Cut out ✂

Cut out ✂

Fold forwards

Fold backwards

Cut out ✂

Cut out ✂

Villa-scene Side piece C.   Fold along the dotted line and glue to Strip D.

Fold Forwards & glue to villa floor Strip B.

Fold

Fold

Cut out ✂

Cut out ✂

Cut out ✂

Cut out ✂

Cut out ✂

Cut out ✂

Cut out ✂

Cut out ✂

Cut out ✂

Cut out ✂

Fold backwards

Fold forwards

Fold backwards

Fold forwards

Women on the villa estate wove baskets.

Crops were brought in from the fields in rickety carts.

Stand these figures in the villa courtyard.

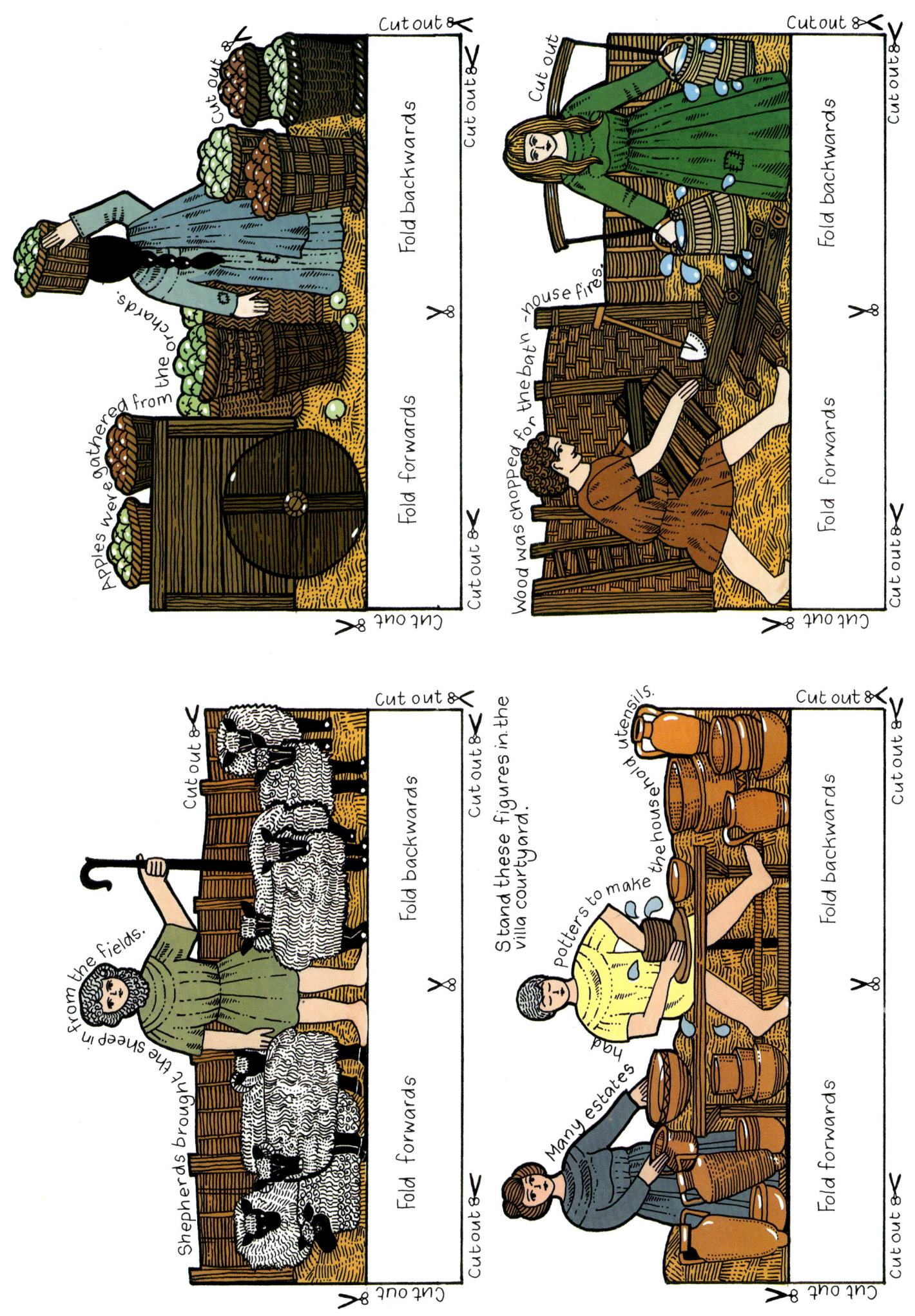

Apples were gathered from the orchards.

Cut out

Fold backwards

Fold forwards

Cut out

Cut out

Cut out

Wood was chopped for the bath-house fires.

Cut out

Fold backwards

Fold forwards

Cut out

Cut out

Shepherds brought the sheep in from the fields.

Cut out

Fold backwards

Fold forwards

Cut out

Cut out

Stand these figures in the villa courtyard.

Many estates had Potters to make the household utensils.

Cut out

Fold backwards

Fold forwards

Cut out

Cut out